A pilgrimage to
The Somme

By Robin Moore

As Remembrance Day approaches in 2016,
Robin Moore endeavours to walk from
Luxembourg to the Somme Battlefields to
commemorate those who fell in The Great War

A pilgrimage to
The Somme

By Robin Moore

This endurance walk from Luxembourg to Albert was completed
by Remembrance Day 2016 to commemorate those who fell in the
Battle of the Somme.

Starting at Luxembourg City the walk takes in part of Belgium and the Somme Valley where Kitchener's Army fought in 1916.

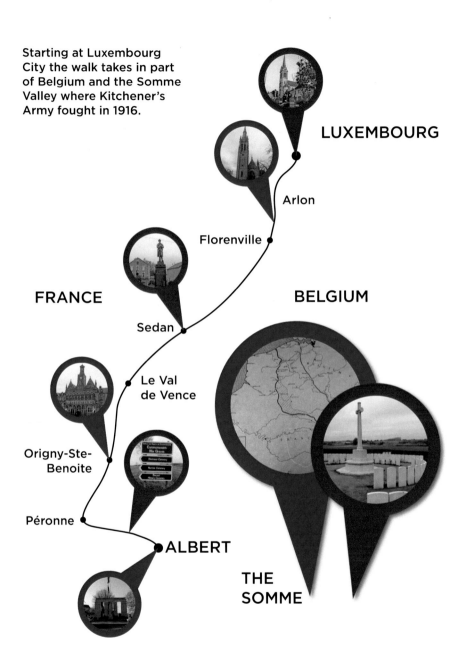

LUXEMBOURG

Arlon

Florenville

FRANCE

BELGIUM

Sedan

Le Val de Vence

Origny-Ste-Benoite

Péronne

ALBERT

THE SOMME

Published October 2017.

FOREWORD

Poem – Kitchener's Army of 'Pals'

The Great War rages on with the reaper as its guide,
Hovering in the theatre of battle to visit death upon each side,
And as the allies push toward the banks of the River Somme,
They find another road to hell amid shell, barbed wire and bomb.

The whisper of the Somme ushered forth more men in boots,
Young, fit and keen to fight are Lord Kitchener's new recruits,
Old pals from 'Blighty', so happy and cheerful they once did roam,
Soon to embrace the wrath of conflict, many miles from home.

Summer marches on as The Battle of Albert draws near,
Beneath the mask of laughter and fun is a sense of growing fear,
Generals speak bold words of gallantry, duty and ultimate victory,
Could anything possibly halt this great surge of equanimity?

Onward march Kitchener's men in hearty voice and cheer,
To the front they go, their songs and anthems clear,
Dawn approaches fast, with the big guns soon to stop,
And for the old pals to fix bayonets, ready to go over the top.

There's no time to think of the day to come,
Still young with cool air and rising sun,
Gone is the life that we once knew,
Replaced by bullet, barbed wire and spew.

60,000 fell on that first morning of battle,
Pushed over the top like herds of cattle,
Summer long fighting saw a million dead,
In a bloodbath of youth who were badly mislead.

Today, a land of white tablets tell of shortness of life,
From Maricourt to Albert where conflict was rife,
Like a bridge spanning nations helping the world to cope,
It's now a place of remembrance, peace and great hope.

By Robin Moore

THE LAND ON WHICH
THIS CEMETERY STANDS
IS THE FREE GIFT
OF THE BELGIAN PEOPLE
FOR THE PERPETUAL RESTING PLACE
OF THOSE OF THE ALLIED ARMIES
WHO FELL IN THE WAR OF 1914-1918
AND ARE HONOURED HERE

A Pilgrimage of WW1

Walking from Luxembourg to Albert (the Somme)

Day 1 Luxembourg to Arlon - 30km

After a late evening lift with "Coppice Derek" to Exeter Airport; a plane to Manchester and another to Luxembourg, I arrive with the help of public transport at the railway station in the city centre where I completed last year's walk from Arnhem, September 2015.

Like the 2014 Pilgrimage of War and Words (now in print), this walk commemorates the Great War and pays tribute to those who fell at the Somme in 1916, which transpired to be one of the bloodiest battles of the conflict. It bears similar poignant reminders of a conflict that changed a way of life engineered through the genius and power of the Industrial Revolution throughout the previous century. The technology devised in this age though sought only to wreak destruction, havoc and hardship.

We wonder how lessons of war have not been learnt despite the fact we are no longer a fledgling society finding our way in the world; on that note I ask why are we still fighting today!

Initially my main battle here amid the traffic is finding the correct route out of the city centre, and after a lot of backtracking with experimental hikes I find myself back at the railway station where I seek help from a local touring company. After receiving clear instructions from the two girls on duty I am on my way wondering why I didn't go there in the first place! Later I seek further assistance from The Bank of Luxembourg who kindly provide me with a local map and confirmation that my journey to Arlon is well underway. Luxembourg itself did not fire a shot in anger during WW1 but was occupied by Germany who used the high ground to shell the French positions, and the rail tracks to infiltrate both France and Belgium. The city today has a look of the modern world yet steeped in gothic-style architecture of yesteryear that is also predominant in parts of France. On my last visit I noticed many refugees around the city centre and a strong police presence at night time. As I walk the streets on this sunny afternoon I see people begging in shop doorways but generally speaking a brisk pace of life continues here devoid of any conflict.

Within an hour the motorway siphons off the traffic reducing the thoroughfare to a gentle ebb, and later I enjoy the comfort of a pavement to the outskirts of the city.

A steel bridge construction ends the Luxembourg experience bringing about a transformation of open countryside broken by small villages. The Autumn is well underway here lacking the riot of colour served up on home shores; instead leaves and twigs drift across the paths obscuring my passage in the dimming light. Facilities become sparse for a while but as dusk approaches I cross into Belgium where the next town awaits on the horizon ahead. Around 6pm I am entering a supermarket in Arlon where I purchase a few groceries, though the place is so big I can't find the bloody exit! Once away from there I hastily look for a night time refuge following a big H sign to the local hospital! Then I walk into a stationary tank next to a memorial in the market square - and so it goes on! After another hour circling the town with no real sense of direction I am fortunate enough to stumble across a lovely little restaurant, The Tulli which also provides accommodation - B&B for 55 Euros.

Day 2 Arlon to Florenville - 24km

Having spent a good night at the Tulli Hotel I start the day with a few photos of the town centre before locating the N40 to Habay. With a population approaching 30,000 Arlon is the smallest provincial capital in Belgium but probably one of the oldest pre-dating Roman Times when its natives were a mix of Celtic and Germanic origin. Sadly it is also known to be one of the first casualties of the Great War when 121 of its town folk were executed on the orders of Colonel Richard Karl von Tessmar. The violation of the 1839 treaty of Belgium Neutrality brought about Britain's involvement in the war and they were soon to take up arms against Germany in the first great battle at Mons Salient, August 23rd 1914.

Having enjoyed a brief encounter with history I locate my route which is reasonable for walking. Enjoying its ruralness I note the transition of opulent gothic buildings of yesterday to those of purpose-built farm dwellings along the way. There are pockets of forest and trees that nature has failed to strip, eminently displaying Autumn colours of golden and reddish brown. Pausing briefly along the way I note a dedication to Notre Dame; derived from the efforts of local people it contains collage, souvenirs and narrative paying tribute to 'Our Lady of Paris'. Arriving at Habay I find little in the way of facilities, so press on through Rulles crossing its diminutive bridge where I see a plaque dedicated to local heroes of the Great War. Later, I make my first stop for coffee at Marbehan where I sit by a wood burner to stay warm and get help with directions from two local guys at the bar. The sun had tried to poke through the haze earlier but I feel has now gone for the rest of the day leaving the cool air to creep in once more. I have completed over 24km and it is 2pm; I will give myself another 4 hours on the road before trying to find lodgings tonight.

Leaving the village on the N891 I set off for Rossignol and Jamoigne but amazingly rain sets in to make a task of it. The road too has its shortcomings with potholes soon filling up with water and I feel a visit from ARC is overdue! I make an excursion to Izel in the hope of seeking out its much-lauded hotel/restaurant, only to later find it closed! A further hike sees me to Pin and with the time at 5pm dusk is approaching already. It's five more 'clicks' to Florenville where I need to find both food and shelter having not eaten since breakfast. On reaching the town my fortune changes as I book into the newly opened Le Florentin Hotel, where the pretty receptionist sets up my wifi and directs me to the nearest supermarket.

Florenville, a substantial town of nearly 6,000 inhabitants, is situated on the Semois River and is close to the French border, which all being well, I will cross in the morning. Then a town or so later, on reaching Mouzon, my past and present pilgrimages of the Great War will meet, thus completing a 6,000km circular trail around France; taking in the Italian border, as far as Geneva and beyond to Verdun, Luxembourg, Lille and Ypres in Belgium. Then back through Vimy Ridge, Arras, Amiens and Nantes; beyond here my travels follow a course through La Rochelle finishing near to the Spanish border at Biarritz.

Day 3 Florenville to Sedan – 40km

Leaving the hotel I pass 'The Church of Our Lady of the Assumption' as I set off in search of the D981 to Mouzon in France. It is a wet start along the quiet forest road and within half an hour I cross the border into France. Nearby on the Belgium side is a statue dedicated to the British war effort during 1914-18 elaborately ornated with a lion at the top. Further on I see a few guys out on a game shoot (hopefully that's all they are interested in!!), and later I pass through the first of several farm villages. Heading into rural France the road becomes more diminutive, interspersed by a handful of tiny communities, and I am relieved to reach the substantial town of Carignan where I enjoy a coffee break.

I have completed 16km already and it is only 11.30am; this place is sizeable though at present looks as though it has been maintained by 'Guy Fawkes', as rubble and broken bits of the thoroughfare lie all around. After skirting round a heap of concrete at the end of town I continue my journey along the D19 to Mouzon.

Traffic speeds by on this slim country road which winds itself around the hilly forest land, but later the sun shines over the River Meuse as I make my descent to the ancient gated town of Mouzon. As I pass through the gateway I am immediately exposed to the beautiful double-towered gothic-style church and after crossing the

Mouzon

Sedan

bridge I find a local restaurant to enjoy a much-needed coffee and a moment to savour my travels in France.

Pressing on in the direction of Sedan I cross over another bridge spanning a wide section of river where two guys are fishing; the air is still and I continue to the end of town. A century ago the terrain along the Meuse would have been a theatre of war taking in the battles of Ardennes, Sedan and Verdun; the latter raging on throughout the entire conflict. It took until 1917 onwards when a US/Franco offensive under General Pershing began to erode the German lines eventually pushing them back through Luxembourg. Beyond the town the country vista opens up again as my route bears down on a peaceful Meuse. The walking pace remains brisk though I gain composure watching the river meander through its quiet, unspoilt landscape, and tiny communities conspicuous only by smoking chimneys. I took a different route to Sedan previously but this undulating terrain allows good all round panoramic views of the whole region including the road on the far side of the river. Passing through new villages I churn up the miles and amuse myself talking in French to cattle and horses; earlier I shared my lunch with a pair of goats whose company brightened up my day. With light still good and a spring in my step I make Sedan by nightfall yielding over 40km due to the longer combination of roads. After a further excursion to Lidl I collect some groceries and later book into a Kyard hotel at 60 Euros for B&B, but had to return to the supermarket having forgotten to get beer! All is good now as I relax and enjoy refreshment with my thoughts drifting to tomorrow and the new adventures that lie in wait.

Day 4 Sedan to Hotel Le Val de Vence - 42km

Sedan was in German occupation throughout the Great War and I am unsure whether it is Remembrance Sunday here in France today but have my poppy attached just in case. After breakfast at the hotel I head off in search of the route to Flize. En route a French hiker assists with directions and the pronunciation of Flize which sounds more like "flees". At the next village I join the cycle route along the River Meuse which runs first to Dom-le-Mesnil which is 6km and a further 2.5km to Flize. The cool air is biting yet the tranquility by the water allows me time to relax away from the stress of the road. I encounter a few cyclists and die-hard joggers along the way; the first section running beside a canal; after a few locks it returns to a fuller expanse flowing alongside woodlands with pastures to my left running back to the road. On reaching Flize I immediately pick up my route to Poix Terron which goes well as far as Bouzincourt. To say this village is a sleepy little place is an understatement - they must be very tired here as I don't remember seeing a soul on the way through let alone anywhere open for trade!

ntre Ville

Zone Industrielle
et Artisanale

Supérette Huit à Huit

D 964

DOUZY   9
SEDAN   17

Ahead the motorway traffic roars in and out of Charleville Méziéres and on reaching the intersection I have difficulty in finding a pedestrian route; after several attempts I follow the only road left, which to my dismay does not have signs for any places on either of my maps. Ah well! Keep bearing right and see what happens is my prognosis! Soon I am on a farm track defined as unsuitable for transport; it is a steep ascent and ahead I see youngsters struggling uphill on their bicycles. They wish me good day and seconds later some maniac speeds past scattering the group though luckily not inflicting casualties. It only takes one idiot to spoil the party! Pressing on the slim lane passes a farm yard as it runs through the rural out backs until all traces of mechanical activity subsides. All that surrounds me is forest now, with its expansive acres, and tons of it!

After continuing for an hour I am heartened by the din of distant traffic and arrive at another unchartered village; guess what – it brings me out onto the D35. Great is my initial response until I realise there are no signs for places anywhere or even nowhere! I toss a coin – left it is then and 5km on I am informed by a pair of local hikers that I now need to turn round and walk 5km back; further more Signy-l'Abbaye, my next destination is 18km! Feeling totally lambasted and with daylight fading rapidly, I hasten past the village from where I had joined the road earlier. A few km later I stop to repair my feet and eat a curled up sandwich salvaged from breakfast time. As dusk looms ever near I march on to Launois-sur-Vence arriving at the D27 junction for Signy which is now only 11km. Amazingly, to my great relief, is a hotel literally across the road from the junction and within moments I am installed in a lovely little room with a breakfast booked for the morning! What a miraculous end to a testing day – it was as if it had been planted there, and words can't describe how grateful I am for that!

Day 5 Hotel Le Val de Vence to Montcornet Region – 58km

Having enjoyed a great rest and slumber I take breakfast before heading off in the direction of Signy-l'Abbaye. It's a murky start with an air of 'Monday Morning Syndrome' which does not bother me particularly as each day is the same in this game. Throughout the early steps the clearing mist is cool and I benefit from the continued quietness of my journey amid forest and farmland which still captures a semblance of endless rusticity.

Ironically all that passes by are two "Convoi Exceptionalle" illustrating that quiet country lanes are the best routes to transport heavy goods in France. At Dommery I stop by a fishing lake and savour a moment of peace; the village has a few interesting buildings which enables me to make sense of the title 'Route of Churches and Fortifications' as it is known to the tourists who frequent it. On arriving at Signy-l'Abbaye I stop for coffee and then go in search of the Tourist Office to obtain a better map.

I find the town disappointing paying over £4 for a basic coffee and no sign of a Tourist Office for assistance. Passing through several more villages I savour the beauty of Autumnal colours along this peaceful byway knowing that a route change is imminent. This I find at the next town signposted as D978 around 1.30pm but without further addition to the 25km walked today, I break for coffee and a chat with the proprietor who enjoys looking through books of my past adventures; then as a gesture of respect treats me to a chocolate desert.

After the interval I cross to the left of the road and commence my journey to Rozoy-sur-Serre.

The walk goes well and I make my destination by nightfall; although when I find the hotel it has a notice saying closed on 7th November - how typical is that - the only bloody day of the year too!

This now means a night trek, which is likely to include camping. It is hazardous despite sporting fluorescent cloths and torch but 2 hours later I reach Montcornet which - guess what - also has no facilities! I see a young maid walking her dog using a ridiculously long lead which I manage to trip over several times as I walk the thoroughfare. After a while we stop and chat; then she tries to help by explaining that I need to take the right fork out of town. Following her instructions I walk a further 3km beyond the fork, finding a spot to pitch my tent in a nearby forest - a short distance from a railway crossroads.

Day 6 Montcornet Region to Origny-Sainte-Benoite - 57km

It is no joke pitching a tent in total darkness in the confines of a thicket! Amazingly I got some sleep but wake to find fog; also my phone has failed to charge up at my previous stay so I have no communication/alarm clock etc. It is an awful struggle in the fog on what now transpires to be a 'truckers route' – not good, and it is a slow 13km yomp to Marle where I do at least obtain a coffee and instructions how to find St Quentin. No sign posts yet but have been informed it is another 50km! The market square is a hive of activity and I capture a moment watching townsfolk exchange hugs as they squeeze past street traders clinging to their baguettes and sweet bread. Passing along the industrial byways is less invigorating though, as I concentrate hard to ensure I arrive at the appropriate junction.

Managing to get out of the town I continue along my route feeling no more animated than I did on arrival there! With no facilities available I rest by some hay bales to eat a tin of mackerel, my only remaining source of nutrition. While nourishing myself the farmer arrives on a forklift needing to distribute the very bale I'm sat on - unbelievable! After moving to another haystack I change my socks before continuing this enduring hike. Setting off again the farmer returns to collect more fodder and we wave goodbye on parting in different directions. Eventually I reach a small village which also brings about another route change; no let up in traffic though as heavy goods wagons, mostly shipping sugar beet from local farms, continue to dominate the highway.

I make it to the next main town Origny-Ste-Benoite and to my delight I see a sign for St Quentin - only 6 km. It is dusk now and I fail once more to find accommodation in this industrial set up. Feeling frustrated by the lack of facilities over the last 100km I depart against the teatime traffic and the sickly smell of sugar beet - walking until I can take no more! Finding a coppice beside the busy highway I retire to pitch a tent as rain comes in to ensure an uncomfortable night. The hope of a hot meal still seems a very long way off!

Day 7 Origny-Sainte-Benoite to Péronne (Somme Region) - 43km
"Il fait mauvais temps ici"

Heavy rain soaked the coppice last night as I heard horses struggle for shelter nearby, but despite a rough 2 days I slept adequately though footsore on the start of today. The weather is unrelenting and so are the trucks - I wonder if there are any left in France!

My plight is halted momentarily at St Quentin where I stop at the first cafe I come to and warm myself up with a coffee. Next I need a sock change and head off to find a suitable shelter.

Later I visit the town centre which has many opulent buildings and for a change hotels! The market square is hosting a live presentation which is well attended despite the rain. St Quentin, largely recognised through its association with art, had seen plenty of action throughout WW1; initially it is remembered as a haven for those retreating from Mons and the Battle of Le Cateau; then more significantly in 1918 at the Battle of St Quentin Canal. This was a pivotal battle starting on 29th September under Australian General John Molash commanding British, American and Australian forces in a final assault on the Hindenburg Line, Germany's most fortified position. It took nearly a million shells in 24 hours to break through the line, but it meant there was little hope of Germany winning the war and from here the allies, further mechanised with tanks, gathered strength in their quest for supremacy in the field.

Stopping at an Ibis Hotel the receptionist helps me book accommodation at Péronne which is a further 30km as I feel another night in the forest would not bode well.

Great I think initially, but later realise I have left the town via the route to Cambrai! Basically I now need to walk the whole way back beyond the town bridge that I crossed 2 hours ago. It is difficult as there are no signs for Péronne and it takes ages until I see one for Amiens. Having asked a good range of people on my way back through the city I eventually get onto the road to Amiens.

Still snowed under with lorries - must have passed a million by now! Worse still is the mini hurricane that comes from nowhere! The dark clouds move quickly with bursts of ice rain, and there is danger as I am tossed into the road like a rag doll. There are no forests here to offer protection and I notice that cars too are struggling to cope with these conditions. For a while it is difficult to make any headway and I wonder if I will ever get to Péronne. Eventually I reach the Somme border and as dusk descends quickly I turn off the Amiens Road and on towards Péronne. Teatime traffic slows me down along another narrow road, but I arrive unscathed by 7pm, collect groceries and then retire to the pre-booked St Claude Hotel costing 70 Euros. Thank God!

Day 8 Péronne to Albert – 26km

Setting off from the St Claude Hotel in Péronne I backtrack through the town to the Albert sign where I commence my journey through the old Somme battlefields. Péronne like St Quentin saw plenty of action during the campaign having been occupied from August 28th, 1914, and on 1st September 1918, a month before the partial destruction of the Hindenburg Line, the enemy was ousted for good - paving the way clear for victory. Today the sky is clear and the calmness of the morning allows me to progress more effectively than yesterday. The road is kinder too with less traffic to dodge and I pause along the way to admire the remaining landmarks of the journey. Beyond the A Route to Arras and Lille there are many war graves and cenotaphs interspersed all the way to Albert. Passing through the rural landscape I hear gunshots nearby; a century ago the heart would have raced but today only pheasants run the risk of defeat! Stopping briefly at Maricourt I visit a cemetery used after an early Somme offensive in August 1916. This was also the last outpost of the British Frontline and from here the French continued their trenches along the Meuse through Verdun extending as far as Basel in Switzerland. Stopping again a few km further on at a small cenotaph I note signs for a Devonshire Cemetery and Commonwealth sites at Rancourt and Bray. As Albert looms ever near the endless fields of white gravestones evoke a chilling reminder of the great debt owed to the British Empire. On reaching the city there is a French Cemetery and just beyond a Police Station. Further on I pass the local Commonwealth Cemetery and after reaching the memorial cenotaph I am fortunate enough to book a room at a local hotel opposite. Once settled in I hurry out to visit the War Museum which is an underground experience full of interest containing many artifacts and history of the Great War and the front line at Albert. Tomorrow I will observe the silence at the city memorial; then catch a train to Lille where I can make my journey home.

EPITAPH

Day 9 Remembrance Day 11/11/2016 - Albert

Today is spent en route with the local band procession as we make our way round Commonwealth, French and British Cemeteries paying tribute to those who gave their lives in the field of battle to set others free. It is also about recognising the importance of wearing a poppy as a symbol of peace. After all it is not the fault of those who died here in battle a century ago that humanity has failed to learn about the futility of war; the evidence here suggests this would have been one of the harshest lessons dealt up on a military scale. Working class people from many nations were sacrificed by the ruling classes for their own financial and political ends. Many of the young men who fought here were part of 'Kitchener's Army', a brigade of friends and families from villages all around the UK stiffened up with a few 'old regulars' from the BEF. Thrust into battle by generals schooled in Crimea War tactics, the Battle of the Somme became known as the worst military disaster in British History.

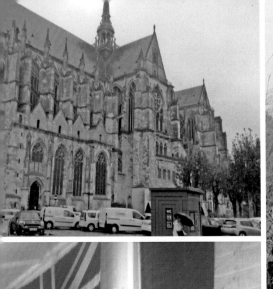

EN SOUVENIR
DU 363 R 1
COMBATS DU 7

This week-long walk completes a Trilogy of expeditions retracing the footsteps of those who fought and died in The Great War in the name of freedom.

Wear your poppy with pride and remember these young lads marched to their deaths in the name of freedom; I hope one day humanity will find a more peaceful path to tread.

To find out more about Robin Moore's past expeditions, (30,000 miles of walks), recent literature, how to support a charity and all fundraising events please visit:

🌐 www.robin-moore.co.uk

f facebook.com/WalkingForCharity

🐦 @RobinMooreWalks

▶ Robin Moore Walking on YouTube

To honour our war history and fallen soldiers please continue to wear a poppy each year and understand that it represents peace. You can also make a donation at any of the charity pages listed on the website above.

Thank You

WAR SERVICE AT 14
A Dedication to Robin Moore's Grandfather, Charles Maurice Thurlby. Possibly at one time during the war he was the youngest serving soldier, joining up with the 4th Battalion of the Northamptonshire Territorials on April 25th, 1915, at the age of 14. He also served with the South Wales Borderers and on Armistice Day was still 18 days off his 18th birthday.

He also served in Ireland and again in WW2.

PHOTOGRAPHS
This book contains pictures of cemeteries and battle fields compiled from walks in France and Belgium to illustrate the horrific reality of WW1. A few pictures were also donated by fellow War Historian Gary Hill.